DREAM
BIG

DREAM BIG

a **5**-
minute

GOAL
JOURNAL

KARL W. GRUBER

ALTHEA
PRESS

Interior and Cover Designer: Stephanie Mautone
Art Producer: Michael Hardgrove
Editor: Sean Newcott
Production Editor: Andrew Yackira
Illustrations: ©Vectorlibellule/Dreamstime.com; AzmariDigitals/Creative Market; FourLeafLover/Creative Market; Minkina/Creative Market.

ISBN: Print 978-1-64152-763-7

this journal belongs to:

_____

CONTENTS

INTRODUCTION

Earl Nightingale once stated, "Everything begins with an idea," and that sentiment applies perfectly to you coming to this journal, ready to focus on and track your goals and dreams. The fact that you have this journal in front of you is a good indicator that you are ready to do this. Give yourself permission to move forward with all of your highest aspirations, pour yourself into these pages to gain perspective, and really believe your goals will manifest in your life.

The beauty of this journal is that it does not require a lot of time from your busy life. *Five minutes a day* is all you need to unleash the power of your thoughts and ideas to focus on what it is you wish to create in your life. If you feel inspired to journal longer, follow that feeling, but just five minutes can work wonders.

Think of this journal as a customizable blueprint to success. It progresses in a way that allows you to organize your thoughts, gain greater clarity, meditate on your goals, and take positive, productive action toward manifesting your dreams into the reality of your life. This is achieved through the five sections that set up your success, each of which builds upon the other.

Sections one through four provide powerful prompts to help you contemplate and define your goals and feel inspired to pursue them. Guided questions and reflections coupled with the power of writing down your intentions will help you reconcile any doubts about how to proceed on this journey. Section five, dedicated to journaling about your goals and the positive steps you are taking to achieve them, increases the power of your highest aspirations through motivational prompts, writing, visualization, and meditation.

SECTION ONE: Clarify Your Ideas *is where you'll define and record the specifics of your goals.*

SECTION TWO: Affirm Your Possibilities *is where you do just that—affirm that your goals as described in section one are attainable. It's where everything starts to come together.*

SECTION THREE: Strategize for Success *teaches you the very real, inherent power of formulating step-by-step written plans and holding yourself accountable to them.*

SECTION FOUR: Express Your Gratitude *offers a place to reflect on and focus on manifesting your goals, fueling positive, creative energy toward their achievement.*

SECTION FIVE: I Can & I Will *comprises the bulk of this journal. Here, for just five minutes on a daily basis, you'll utilize goal-achieving prompts and meditate on inspirational quotes to focus your intentions on the* **whys, hows,** *and* **whens** *of making your dreams a reality.*

Remember, your goals are unique to you, and no dream or aspiration is too big or too small. If your goals change or you want to revisit your approach to them, then do just that. You can change or modify sections of this journal to make them fit what you need. No matter what, don't be afraid to go after what you want.

As you write daily in this journal, savor little moments here and there to enjoy achieving the highest and best version of you that is possible.

"The future belongs to those who believe in the beauty of their dreams."

—ELEANOR ROOSEVELT

SECTION ONE

Clarify Your Ideas

CONGRATULATIONS! You've taken that first, all-important, step toward creating a clear-cut plan to accomplish your highest aspirations, dreams, and goals! There is great power in writing down that which you desire in your life: a power this journal will help you develop. Your goal with regard to journaling is to take time—maybe for the first time—to develop a crystal clear, high-definition picture of exactly what it is you wish to be, do, or have. As you develop your focus and write out your goals, remember you—*only you!*— have the power to create the life you desire. You are the writer, producer, editor, and director of your life—no one else. *Believe in yourself—always.*

Nothing is too big or too small for you to consider. It is, after all, your life, so go for it all right here in these pages. This journal is your opportunity to unburden yourself from any perceived limitations or restraints you feel, and reflect on the strength and determination you already possess to meet any challenges on the path toward success.

Consider the following prompts to help you gain clarity on what you want to achieve.

What goals and dreams have you delayed pursuing because others don't approve, or long-held beliefs won't allow you to?

_____

_____

_____

_____

_____

_____

_____

_____

Your very real happiness and fulfillment are your ultimate goals. How can you remove the obstacles (others' disapproval, your own beliefs, etc.) in the way of achieving your goals?

_____

_____

_____

_____

_____

_____

_____

_____

_____

How does it make you feel knowing you have the freedom
to pursue your greatest dreams and goals?

_____

_____

_____

_____

_____

_____

_____

_____

_____

_____

In answering these questions, you've engaged the power of
journaling plus high-definition visualization to define the
life you want to live. With this newfound clarity, take a few
moments to sit in and really feel your power. Write down how
you feel so you can bring up that feeling again in the future.

_____

_____

_____

_____

_____

_____

_____

_____

_____

SECTION TWO

Affirm Your Possibilities

WITH SOME DEFINITION now about exactly what you want to accomplish, it is time to affirm those goals to help you overcome any feelings (conscious or unconscious) of unworthiness that may have previously kept you from achieving them. Many people can feel intimidated and afraid to actualize their biggest goals, because of the fear of failure or disappointing others. This is your time to leave those feelings behind. Now that you know and believe that your goals are indeed achievable, you can hold yourself accountable for making them happen.

Each time you write in this journal you affirm the very real possibilities in your life, and gain power knowing there is no limit to them. While it is true that you must develop a clear plan and put in the time and effort to achieve the plan's goals, once in motion, the magic will happen.

Consider these prompts to affirm your goals.

Thinking about your goals, which of your talents and abilities can help you achieve and manifest them? What other resources and people are available that you can tap into to make this a reality?

With your new clarity and affirmation of what you want to achieve in life, what new and wonderful things can you imagine enjoying or pursuing through your goals and dreams?

As writing down your goals has great power to help you commit, so too does visualization and meditation of your powers. Create a personal mantra to affirm your best qualities. Consider statements like, "I am smart;" "I will work hard to achieve my dreams;" "I deserve this;" and "I know what I want." What is your mantra?

SECTION THREE

✦ —————————————— ◈ —————————————— ✦

Strategize for Success

IT'S ONE THING to have goals and dreams; we all do. But for many of us, our goals remain elusive—something desired, yet not attained. One way to bring your goals to fruition is to formulate an actionable plan. To use a simple analogy: You are the captain of your ship. As captain, you have a destination in mind, but without charting a precise course, it's unlikely you will arrive at your exact destination. Without a charted course—your map, so to speak—your ship will drift, subject to the whims of the currents and waves, aimless and off course.

Creating a plan of action greatly increases the likelihood of attaining your goals. It's a written reminder of what's important and the steps you've committed to take, prioritizing how you'll spend your time.

But no plan is set in stone; every captain adjusts for the various factors that can throw a journey off course. Don't be afraid to revisit sections one and two, at any time, to refine and redefine your goals to suit your current or future needs. Be flexible, but stay focused, stay positive, and continue to believe you will achieve your goals.

Now that you've defined your goals, it's time to prioritize them. Create a numbered list (1 being most important) of your goals.

1.

2.

3.

4.

5.

Starting with your number one goal, what specific steps will you take to reach it?

Visualize yourself having successfully achieved your goals. As you do so, write down how that makes you feel (happy, joyful, excited, proud, motivated, etc.).

SECTION FOUR

Express Your Gratitude

ONE OF YOUR GREATEST powers is the ability to feel and express gratitude.

Think back to when you first mapped out your highest aspirations. Compare that to where you are now. Meditate on all that you love and appreciate in your life today and let your gratitude flow freely. Every time you express gratitude for something, more of what you are grateful for may come your way.

Journaling is a dynamic method for taking stock of where you are versus where you want to be, and expressing gratitude for all the experiences, influences, people, and things that have brought you to this point—of dreaming big and attaining your goals.

Think of all the people who have helped and inspired you along the way. This is your opportunity to express your gratitude for their influence and to continue to move proactively toward the successful manifestation of your dream life. It won't take you very long to uncover the power of gratitude as you work through your *Dream Big* journal.

Take a close look at your life and write down three things you are most grateful for—they can be people, situations, experiences, etc.

1.

2.

3.

Considering those things you've identified you are grateful for, describe why you are grateful. What have they contributed to your life? Your goals? How will you express your gratitude to them?

Focusing on the goals you have set, let yourself be grateful for them as if they have already been achieved. What does this look and feel like to your future self?

SECTION FIVE

I Can & I Will

THIS SECTION of your journal is your opportunity to take five minutes a day to focus on, honor, and work toward your goals. The prompts in this section will continue to guide you on the path to clarifying your ideas, affirming your possibilities, strategizing for long-term success, expressing your gratitude throughout your journey, and ultimately achieving the goals that you have been dreaming of and working hard for. This is your time to increase the power of your intentions and bring your ultimate goals into the spotlight. While this journal allows you to "Dream Big," in this section, *you* can & *you* will uncover your power to achieve those dreams.

Enjoy the journey and never stop dreaming.

> *"... it sometimes seems that intense desire creates not only its own opportunities, but its own talents."*
> —ERIC HOFFER

What goal is your number one priority right now?

_____

_____

What three actionable steps can you take today to help move you toward that goal?

1. _____
2. _____
3. _____

Where there's a will, there's a way. What resources are available to you now?

_____

_____

Which of your beliefs is most beneficial to achieving success?

_____

_____

What are you grateful for today? Why?

_____

_____

_____

"... small opportunities are often the beginning of great enterprises."

—DEMOSTHENES

What two ways can you simplify the definition of your biggest goal to be more specific about the results?

1. _____

2. _____

List three simple steps you can take today to make progress toward your goals.

1. _____

2. _____

3. _____

Which of your talents and expertises can you use to advance toward success?

_____

_____

List any wins—big or small—you have achieved so far on your journey to your goal(s).

1. _____

2. _____

3. _____

How has your attitude toward your goals changed for the better?

_____

_____

_____

Visualize achieving your biggest goal right
now. How does that make you feel?

_____

_____

_____

How will you and those around you benefit from your achievement?

_____

_____

_____

How have your emotions changed in the pursuit of your goals?

_____

_____

_____

Where do you see yourself one year from now?

_____

_____

_____

What actions—big or small—can you take
today to help realize your goals?

_____

_____

_____

"Man's mind, once stretched by a new idea, never regains its original dimensions."
—OLIVER WENDELL HOLMES JR.

What is your timeline for the achievement of your number one goal?

_____

_____

_____

Remember to be grateful every day.
What are you grateful for today?

_____

_____

_____

Upon achieving your biggest goal,
how do you see your life changing?

_____

_____

_____

List three ways you envision feeling once these goals manifest.

1. _____
2. _____
3. _____

What untapped abilities can you put into
play to help reach your goals?

_____

_____

_____

DATE _____

"The quality of a person's life is in direct
proportion to their commitment to excellence,
regardless of their chosen field of endeavor."
—VINCE LOMBARDI

How have your goals changed or shifted, if at
all, since beginning this journey?

_____
_____

List the three most motivating things spurring
you on to achieve your goals.

1. _____
2. _____
3. _____

Write down how you envision things will be
when you realize your dreams.

_____
_____

What five-minute strategy can you unleash
today to make your goals reality?

_____
_____

List the progress you've made toward your
goals. What are you most proud of?

1. _____
2. _____
3. _____

"Preceding accomplishment must be desire. Thy desires must be strong and definite."

– GEORGE S. CLASON

Reaffirm your powerful desire to reach your goals.

1. _____

2. _____

3. _____

You are the sole creator of your life—what beautiful things do you see yourself creating?

_____

_____

_____

It's been said, "Change yourself to change your world." What changes have you made for the better?

_____

_____

_____

What tools for creating your goals might you be overlooking?

_____

_____

_____

Write down any new or increased feelings of worthiness you have recently experienced.

_____

_____

_____

"Obstacles are those frightful things you see when you take your eyes off your goals."

—HENRY FORD

Which unexpected sources have provided help with achieving your goals?

_____

_____

Since you started journaling, have you formulated any new goals? List them here.

1. _____

2. _____

3. _____

How will you integrate any newly emerged goals into your overall manifestation strategy?

_____

_____

Write down the most inspirational thoughts that keep you on track toward your goals.

_____

_____

How do you feel you've changed since you created a plan to achieve success?

_____

_____

What resources do you intend to tap into today that can help you achieve your goals and dreams?

_____

_____

_____

Are there any fears or doubts that have faded since you've taken action to pursue your goals?

_____

_____

_____

Harness the power of gratitude by listing all you are currently grateful for.

1. _____

2. _____

3. _____

What feelings of limitation have you let go of during your journaling process?

_____

_____

_____

Take a moment to meditate on the unique beauty of your goals and dreams. How does that make you feel?

_____

_____

_____

"Desire is the key to motivation..."
—MARIO ANDRETTI

*Write down three powerful, positive affirmations that
will help you stay on track to achieve your goals.*

1. _____

2. _____

3. _____

*Record three steps you'll take to demonstrate
the affirmations you just created.*

1. _____

2. _____

3. _____

*What limiting beliefs do you need to release
to move closer to your goals?*

_____

_____

_____

*Thinking about your number one goal, what about
achieving it makes you feel happiest?*

_____

_____

_____

What are you grateful for now that you previously overlooked?

_____

_____

_____

Focused pursuit of achievement requires flexibility. What, if anything, has changed regarding your defined goals?

_____

_____

_____

_____

Always be aware of any wins that come your way. What are you most proud of today?

_____

_____

_____

When thinking about your goals, what brings a smile to your face?

_____

_____

_____

Of all of your goals and dreams, which do you feel the most excited to reach?

_____

_____

_____

How has concentrating on your number one goal changed your overall priorities?

_____

_____

_____

_____

"You see things; and you say 'Why?' But I dream things that never were; and I say 'Why not?'"
—GEORGE BERNARD SHAW

*How can you practice the habit of a success
mindset to reach your goals?*

_____
_____
_____

*Since starting this journey, how have you progressed in your
belief that your highest aspirations can come true?*

_____
_____
_____

*Give yourself full permission to imagine the joy of
successfully attaining your goals. How does it feel?*

_____
_____

*How can you build on your belief in your goals, now
that you're on a direct path to achieving them?*

_____
_____

With your goals in mind, finish this sentence, "It will be nice if … !"

_____
_____
_____

Write down three new ideas to help make your goals a reality.

1. _____

2. _____

3. _____

Allow yourself to feel as though you have achieved your top goal(s).
Complete this statement: "I love how it feels when…"

_____

_____

_____

_____

What three things are you grateful for today?

1. _____

2. _____

3. _____

What recent actions or thoughts have you had that
demonstrate you are in control of creating your ideal life?

_____

_____

_____

What did you/will you do today to hold yourself
accountable for your ultimate success?

_____

_____

_____

"Never give in, except to convictions of honour and good sense."
—WINSTON CHURCHILL

Name three reasons you are committed to
making your dreams a reality.

1. _____

2. _____

3. _____

How does the thought of your goals coming to fruition make you feel?

_____

_____

_____

What has changed for the better since you
committed to reaching your goals?

_____

_____

_____

With your goal achievements in mind, complete
this sentence, "I'm in the process of…"

_____

_____

_____

What can you do to empower yourself today?

_____

_____

_____

What positive thoughts can you affirm here to bring
you closer to the reality of your dreams?

_____

_____

_____

_____

What one belief can you change to help make goal attainment easier?

_____

_____

_____

_____

_____

Remind yourself why you want to pursue your greatest goal(s).

_____

_____

_____

_____

Why are you worthy of receiving your greatest desires?

_____

_____

_____

_____

How do you see yourself celebrating the happy
occasion of reaching your goals?

_____

_____

_____

_____

DATE _____

*What thought pattern can you tweak to boost
your chances of achieving your top goals?*

_____

_____

_____

*What one action can you take right now to
make progress toward success?*

_____

_____

*What would happen if you gave yourself permission
to be the happy recipient of your biggest goals?*

_____

_____

How does it make you feel to imagine your goals are your reality?

_____

_____

_____

Upon the realization of your biggest dream, how would you celebrate?

_____

_____

_____

"Paralyze resistance with persistence."
—WOODY HAYES

Describe the powerful picture you have in mind regarding your goals.

_____

_____

_____

_____

What positive shift within you, regarding
your dream life, have you noticed?

_____

_____

_____

Why do you feel your goals are meant to be?

_____

_____

_____

What is the most compelling reason you believe
you will achieve what you desire?

_____

_____

_____

How do you think you will change when
your goals become your reality?

_____

_____

_____

DATE _____

Will having your goals become reality give you a sense of peace?

_____

_____

_____

_____

Who or what influenced you to move confidently toward your goals?

_____

_____

_____

_____

Who would you like to share your victories with?

_____

_____

_____

Name five past successes that can help you now.

1. _____
2. _____
3. _____
4. _____
5. _____

On a scale of 1 to 10, how strong is your desire
to realize your goals today?

_____

_____

_____

_____

*On a scale of 1 to 10, how strongly do you believe
you deserve to achieve your goals?*

_____

_____

_____

How can you increase this belief?

_____

_____

_____

*Accountability and productivity go hand in hand for goal
achievement. What have you done today to make your goals a reality?*

_____

_____

_____

*What thoughts would give you permission to
enjoy the ride toward your goals?*

_____

_____

_____

*Have you put pressure on yourself to make your
goals possible? How can you release it?*

_____

_____

_____

What is a new belief you can embrace to make your dreams come true?

How will this new belief increase the likelihood of creating your goals?

Based on your new powerful belief, what action can you take to move toward your goals?

On a scale of 1 to 10, how do you feel about your progress toward acquiring the reality of your dreams?

How would you like to improve your progress?

"Whatever the mind can conceive and believe, the mind can achieve."

—NAPOLEON HILL

Identify any resistant feelings you have toward the attainment of your goals and the reasons you should release those feelings.

_____

_____

_____

Now, release these feelings. Enjoy the lightness of having that burden lifted. How does it feel?

_____

_____

_____

What are the biggest rewards you will receive once you achieve your goals?

_____

_____

_____

Who will you share these rewards with?

_____

_____

_____

Take this moment to embrace and resonate with the joy of the journey toward your goals. How do you feel?

_____

_____

DATE _____

Name three things you are grateful for today.

1. _____
2. _____
3. _____

What is the biggest, most positive change you've noticed in yourself since you started actively pursuing your goals?

_____
_____
_____
_____

What can you do today to amplify your chances of success?

_____
_____
_____

What would it mean if you could simply trust that your goals will be achieved?

_____
_____
_____

How can you change any negative thoughts you are holding on to in order to maintain alignment with your goals?

_____
_____
_____

List three positive thoughts you can adopt in
service of striving for your goals.

1. _____

2. _____

3. _____

What is the most powerful, positive thought
you can reach for right now?

_____

_____

Thinking as though your goals are a reality, what three "as though"
statements can you imagine will move you closer to success?

1. _____

2. _____

3. _____

Have you noticed any new abilities as you
persist in reaching your goals?

_____

_____

List five ways you feel more confident since
becoming determined to attain your dreams.

1. _____

2. _____

3. _____

4. _____

5. _____

"The only thing that stands between a man and what he wants from life is often merely the will to try it and the faith to believe that it is possible."

—DAVID VISCOTT

List five thoughts that make you feel good about having your goals become your reality.

1. _____
2. _____
3. _____
4. _____
5. _____

Focus on your value and worthiness. How do you define it? How does this make you feel?

_____

What is the greatest change you wish to see in yourself once you've attained your goals?

_____

What can you do right now to bring your goals closer to reality?

_____

Silence any doubts or fears that have held you back from achieving your goals in the past. How does that make you feel?

_____

*What breakthroughs or insights have come
to you since you started journaling?*

_____

_____

*How can you apply lessons learned from your biggest
accomplishment in life to achieving your goals?*

_____

_____

*Free your imagination and write down the love, fun, and
joy you will have when your dreams are your reality.*

_____

_____

*Be bold, imaginative, and dream big: Can
you aim higher with your goals?*

_____

_____

*Write passionately and expressively about
what it will be like to live your ideal life.*

_____

_____

Imagine your future self, living the life you
have always dreamed of. What advice would
that future self offer you now?

_____

_____

_____

_____

In one sentence, describe what your successful self looks and feels like.

_____

_____

_____

Take a moment to connect with the most empowered,
successful, and happy version of yourself—what
does that version feel like day to day?

_____

_____

What lessons from your successful, happy self can you
use to move closer to the reality of your dreams?

_____

_____

What will you feel when you have achieved all of your dreams?

_____

_____

_____

*What progress did you experience recently that
moved you along the path to your goals?*

_____

_____

_____

_____

*Affirm the reasons you want what you want—to keep you on
track to live the life you love, and love the life you live.*

_____

_____

_____

_____

*Think about each of your goals with all the passion and feeling you
can muster. How does this inspire you to feel they are within reach?*

_____

_____

_____

_____

*What two actions can you take right now to
challenge yourself to achieve your goals?*

1. _____

2. _____

What adjustments have you made on this path to your dreams?

_____

_____

_____

_____

Connect right now with your deepest inner self and see the brilliant sparkle of your greatest hopes and desires. What insights does this give you?

Which of your goals holds the promise of the greatest good for you and your family?

Which of your desires has the most clarity?

Are any of your dreams still a bit hazy? What do you think it will take to bring them into focus?

Has any progress toward your goals come from a surprising source?

What happens when you own your power to achieve your dreams?

_____

_____

_____

_____

Has claiming your power to direct your life changed
your belief in manifesting your dreams?

_____

_____

_____

_____

*As you walk this path of your own power, have any new
goals and desires developed? List them here.*

1. _____

2. _____

3. _____

What obstacles do you need to remove to see your goals more clearly?

_____

_____

_____

_____

Review the road map you created to reach your goals. Do you
feel you are still on course? What will you do to correct, if not?

_____

_____

_____

_____

DATE _____

What are the three most important reasons you feel
you deserve to have your dreams manifest?

1. _____

2. _____

3. _____

How is your successful future self different
from how you see your present self?

_____

_____

Affirm your willingness to do the work toward attaining
your goals. List three things you will do today to help.

1. _____

2. _____

3. _____

Knowing that old grudges can block momentum, are there
any injustices you have been unwilling to forgive?

_____

_____

If you free yourself of these obstacles, is the
path to your goals any clearer?

_____

_____

_____

"Our deepest fear is not that we are inadequate. Our deepest fear is that we are powerful beyond measure."
—MARIANNE WILLIAMSON

List three things you are willing to do to reach your goals. Start each sentence with, "I am willing to..." to affirm your willingness.

1. _____

2. _____

3. _____

What is the simplest, most practical thing you can do today to get closer to your dreams?

_____

_____

Solidify the reality of your desires by focusing intently on them now. What are three ways to do this?

1. _____

2. _____

3. _____

What resources have you yet to tap into to make your goals happen?

_____

_____

_____

Which of your talents have you yet to use to make your goals materialize?

_____

_____

_____

What are two new goals you can reach for
beyond what you want to achieve now?

1. _____
2. _____

Imagine you have achieved all of your goals.
What does this look like?

_____

_____

_____

_____

What would it take to open your mind and heart to embrace
your ultimate success? List three ways you can do this.

1. _____
2. _____
3. _____

Imagine you are now living your ideal life. What does this feel like?

_____

_____

_____

What are three affirmations you can make to
help make your dreams a reality?

1. _____
2. _____
3. _____

*Feel the power of your goals, and the joy and satisfaction
they give you. Describe how this feels.*

_____

_____

_____

Which of your goals do you feel has the most power? Why?

_____

_____

_____

_____

*What is the most encouraging thing that has
happened recently to help you stay on course?*

_____

_____

_____

Do you still feel in alignment with all of your goals?

_____

_____

_____

Which of your goals do you feel will come the easiest to you?

_____

_____

_____

"Always bear in mind that your own resolution to succeed is more important than any other."

—ABRAHAM LINCOLN

*What aspects of your life have you yet to bring
into resonance with your goals?*

_____

_____

_____

*Make sure your goals are in alignment with the integrity, abundance,
and peace you seek. List two things you can do to ensure this occurs.*

1. _____

2. _____

Which of your goals holds the brightest hope for your future self?

_____

_____

_____

What is it about this goal that makes it the brightest?

_____

_____

_____

How does the vision of your goals bring you joy?

_____

_____

What single word is in perfect harmony with your biggest dreams?

*What are the most powerful words you can speak today
to make progress toward your goal success?*

*Where have you yet to look for inspiration to
produce the reality of your dreams?*

*Who do you know who has already achieved what
you desire and what can you learn from them?*

What has been a recent source of inspiration for you?

*Do you have a clear vision of attaining your goals? If not,
how can you gain clarity? What is in your way?*

_____

_____

_____

_____

*Is there any way to further increase your willingness
to receive that which you desire?*

_____

_____

_____

_____

Which of your goals gives you the greatest sense of joy?

_____

_____

_____

*How can you harness this joy to move you farther
along the path to achieving your goals?*

_____

_____

_____

*Remember your dreams are a gift; express
your gratitude for this gift now.*

_____

_____

_____

"Ignore what a man desires and you ignore the very source of his power."
–WALTER LIPPMANN

To find the deeper magic within your desires, take a moment
to contemplate them. What insights did you gain?

_____

_____

_____

_____

How has your journey to your dreams
brought you closer to their reality?

_____

_____

_____

_____

Describe three beautiful aspects of your number one dream.

1. _____

2. _____

3. _____

What single sentence describes the reality of your goals?

_____

_____

_____

_____

What thoughts about your number one goal light you up with joy?

_____

_____

_____

_____

All goals and dreams begin with a thought. What one thought can you hold to increase the likelihood of their manifestation?

_____

_____

_____

What do you feel grateful for today?

_____

_____

_____

Connect with your higher-level self and ask for its wise direction. What does it tell you?

_____

_____

_____

Make a brief list of your goals to keep visible at all times.

1. _____
2. _____
3. _____

What promise does your number one goal hold for you?

_____

_____

_____

*How has this persistent pursuit of your highest-level
aspirations changed you for the better?*

_____

_____

_____

_____

What new, better traits or beliefs have now become a part of you?

_____

_____

_____

_____

*Which of these new traits and beliefs seem to be working
to your advantage in creating your dreams?*

_____

_____

_____

_____

How will further realizing your dreams likely change you?

_____

_____

_____

_____

What does this new you have to offer the world that you didn't before?

_____

_____

_____

_____

"Step out of the history that is holding you back. Step into the new story you are willing to create."
— OPRAH WINFREY

What fears can you release to clear the road to the life you desire and make the way easier?

_____

_____

What can you do right now to align yourself with the successful attainment of your dreams?

_____

Evaluate your progress on achieving your goals. Are any course corrections needed today?

_____

_____

Radiate gratitude for everything connected to your goals. What are you most grateful for today?

_____

_____

Since you've committed to making your dreams happen, what has improved in your life?

_____

_____

*If your goals and dreams turned out even better
than you imagine, how would this feel?*

_____

_____

_____

_____

What would "even better" look like?

_____

_____

_____

_____

What miracle would you like to see happen in your life?

_____

_____

_____

_____

*What are three aspects of your biggest
goal you need more clarity on?*

1. _____

2. _____

3. _____

*What events would you like to make happen today
to bring your dreams closer to you?*

_____

_____

_____

_____

DATE _____

What is the single most important thing you can do
right now to move toward living your ideal life?

_____

_____

_____

With your number one goal in mind, what powerful
symbol represents its importance to you?

_____

_____

_____

When you visualize your ultimate goal, how does that make you feel?

_____

_____

_____

Once you attain this ultimate goal, how will it enhance your life?

_____

_____

_____

What do you feel is the best way to make progress today
toward accomplishing your most ambitious goal?

_____

_____

_____

"Desire creates the power."
—RAYMOND HOLLIWELL

Visualize your biggest goal and describe it as vividly as you can. How does this make you feel?

Imagine it is one year from now, and you are describing how easy it was to achieve your goals. What surprised you most?

Describe your life as you envision it five years from now. Which of your dreams has come true?

Check in on your current progress toward creating your dream life. Are you happy with it?

Even if satisfied with your progress, how could it be better?

List the specifics of what you want to create in your life.
How has this changed from the first time you did this?

1. _____

2. _____

3. _____

Can you imagine something even better than
this? Be specific in the details.

_____

_____

_____

_____

What amount of money, time, or resources
will help you create your ideal life?

_____

_____

_____

_____

List three ways these resources can become
available. Remember, dream big!

1. _____

2. _____

3. _____

What other thoughts and actions can you take
to fly to even greater goal heights?

_____

_____

_____

What are three practical, easy-to-make-happen things you can do today to work toward your success?

1. _____
2. _____
3. _____

What do you expect your greatest dreams will deliver to you?

_____

_____

_____

Is there anything you would like to add to, or delete from, your original list of goals?

_____

_____

_____

What doubts or fears are still holding you back that you need to let go of?

_____

_____

_____

What resource are you grateful for right now that will help you reach your goals?

_____

_____

_____

"Nothing splendid has ever been achieved except by those who dared believe that something inside of them was superior to circumstance."

—BRUCE BARTON

What new belief have you recently acquired?

What hindering old belief have you let go of?

Stand at the mountaintop of your dreams. How does this look and feel?

What sense of peace did you find yesterday or today?

Where did unexpected help come from yesterday or today?

What sense of joy will your completed goals bring you?

_____

_____

_____

_____

How have you shown self-love today?

_____

_____

_____

_____

List three daily habits that keep you focused on your goals.

1. _____
2. _____
3. _____

What characteristics does your biggest dream have?

_____

_____

_____

_____

How has your willingness to receive your desires improved?

_____

_____

_____

_____

DATE _____

*Is there one specific goal that has become
clearer for you? Write it down.*

_____

_____

_____

How has your gratitude increased?

_____

_____

_____

Describe your current level of commitment to your goals today.

_____

_____

_____

*What three things have changed for the better
in your life as you pursue your goals?*

1. _____
2. _____
3. _____

What personal trait or habit can you improve to help meet your goals?

_____

_____

_____

What can you ask for that's even better than what you already desire?

_____

_____

_____

_____

What level of intention and commitment will it take to succeed?

_____

_____

_____

_____

What progress did you make today toward your goals?

_____

_____

_____

Create three goal affirmations to stay the course.

1. _____

2. _____

3. _____

What powerful emotions are working for you?

_____

_____

_____

_____

"Nothing is impossible to a willing heart."
—JOHN HEYWOOD

List two ways you can experience the joys of your goals right now.

1. _____

2. _____

Describe the picture that best represents your dream life.

_____

_____

_____

_____

Check your course. Any adjustments needed?

_____

_____

_____

_____

From what source has surprise support come?

_____

_____

_____

_____

What is your intention for today?

_____

_____

_____

_____

DATE _____

What positive thoughts do you have today?

_____
_____
_____
_____
_____

What three words speak to the success of your goals?

1. _____
2. _____
3. _____

How will success change you?

_____
_____
_____
_____

How has your clear-cut goal setting changed you?

_____
_____
_____

What do you want to happen today and how can you ensure it does?

_____
_____
_____
_____

Why do you believe it is possible to have what you want?

_____

_____

_____

Who, besides you, will benefit from your success?

_____

_____

_____

What would make you happy today?

_____

_____

_____

How has your attitude changed since starting this journal?

_____

_____

_____

How can you make today even more successful?

_____

_____

_____

_____

What three things will you do today to make progress toward success?

1. _____

2. _____

3. _____

Where can you find inspiration today?

_____

_____

_____

_____

_____

Express appreciation for two things you've taken for granted.

1. _____

2. _____

How will you improve today?

_____

_____

_____

_____

*How will you show your gratitude today
for that which you appreciate?*

_____

_____

_____

_____

_____

"For the resolute and determined, there is time and opportunity."

—RALPH WALDO EMERSON

Which of your skills flow easily and effortlessly in the pursuit of your goals?

_____

_____

_____

_____

What inspired you today?

_____

_____

_____

What motivated you today?

_____

_____

_____

How can you increase your determination?

_____

_____

_____

List three beautiful outcomes of your goal success.

1. _____
2. _____
3. _____

How has your confidence increased over the past month?

_____
_____
_____
_____

What wins came your way today?

_____
_____
_____
_____

What would make your heart soar today?

_____
_____
_____

Where can you look for happiness right now?

_____
_____
_____
_____

What makes you hopeful?

_____
_____
_____
_____

In what ways can you aim even higher with your dreams?

_____

_____

_____

Is there room for you to improve? How?

_____

_____

_____

How has your belief in your ultimate success increased?

_____

_____

_____

How has the vision of your success expanded?

_____

_____

_____

What have you overlooked on the road to your success?

_____

_____

_____

"All our dreams can come true, if we have the courage to pursue them."
—WALT DISNEY

How have you changed in the pursuit of your success?

_____

_____

_____

_____

How have your plans changed in the pursuit of your goals?

_____

_____

_____

_____

_____

What would you like to create today?

_____

_____

_____

_____

What would bring you joy today?

_____

_____

_____

What motivates you today?

_____

_____

_____

DATE _____

What new belief do you need to adopt to attract your dreams?

_____

_____

_____

_____

What would bring you more joy today?

_____

_____

_____

*What grudge can you release now to help
clear the way to your ideal life?*

_____

_____

_____

Who or what inspires you today?

_____

_____

_____

Write about three things that will add beauty and joy to your life.

1. _____

2. _____

3. _____

When do you want to achieve your goal successes?

_____
_____
_____
_____

How will it make you a better person when you do?

_____
_____
_____
_____

How will the world benefit from your successes?

_____
_____
_____
_____

*In what way will you feel better about yourself
when your dreams are reality?*

_____
_____
_____
_____

*What word adequately expresses how much
you want to achieve your goals?*

_____
_____
_____

DATE _____

What does success look like to you?

_____

_____

_____

What three actions will you take today to
bring your desires closer to reality?

1. _____

2. _____

3. _____

What phrase can you think of to keep you motivated?

_____

_____

_____

What new things are you grateful for?

_____

_____

_____

Where do you see yourself in one year?

_____

_____

_____

How has the vision of achieving your goals become clearer?

_____
_____
_____
_____

What makes you happy today?

_____
_____
_____
_____

Who can you thank today, and for what?

_____
_____
_____
_____

What would increase your confidence?

_____
_____
_____
_____

Are you happy with your goal progress so far?

_____
_____
_____
_____

DATE _____

What is the most important thing you plan to accomplish today?

_____

_____

_____

_____

What is the biggest reason you want the goals you are striving for?

_____

_____

_____

_____

Where can you look for inspiration today?

_____

_____

_____

_____

Focusing on the big picture of your success,
are you happy with what you see?

_____

_____

_____

_____

Why do you believe that attaining what you
want will bring you happiness?

_____

_____

_____

_____

Name three ways you've grown as a person on this journey.

1. _____
2. _____
3. _____

What delighted you today?

_____
_____
_____
_____
_____

What makes you smile when you think about your success?

_____
_____
_____
_____

What unexpected good things happened today?

_____
_____
_____
_____
_____

Is your view of your life today different than just a few weeks ago?

_____
_____
_____
_____

What would open your heart further to receive your desires?

_____

_____

_____

What is the best thing that happened to you today?

_____

_____

_____

Would more abundance make the path to your goals easier?

_____

_____

_____

Is there anything more you can be grateful for?

_____

_____

_____

*How have other people's views of you changed for
the better as you walk toward your ideal life?*

_____

_____

_____

"Optimism is the faith that leads to achievement."
—HELEN KELLER

What are three ways you can become more prosperous?

1. _____
2. _____
3. _____

What thought best represents your ultimate success?

_____

_____

_____

_____

What two things can you do today to increase
the likelihood of your success?

1. _____
2. _____

What do the power and strength of your
successful future self feel like?

_____

_____

_____

What beautiful thing inspires you to stay the course?

_____

_____

_____

What would make this a wonderful day?

_____

_____

_____

_____

What is the simplest way to stay committed to your goals?

_____

_____

_____

_____

**What makes you feel empowered as you strive
toward your goal achievements?**

_____

_____

_____

_____

Describe your ideal day upon the achievement of your dreams.

_____

_____

_____

_____

**What actor would best play you in a movie
about your dream-fulfilled life?**

_____

_____

_____

What would it take to light up your day today?

_____

_____

_____

How has the pursuit of your ideal life rekindled a spark in you?

_____

_____

_____

_____

What would increase your level of determination?

_____

_____

_____

*In what way can you raise your level of confidence
that your dreams will manifest?*

_____

_____

_____

*What or who appeared in your life today
that increased your gratitude?*

_____

_____

_____

DATE _____

What can you focus on today to allow your dreams to flow easily to you?

_____

_____

_____

_____

What one thought can you reach for today to increase your belief that your ideal life will be yours?

_____

_____

_____

_____

Change your mind, and your results will change. What can you change to increase your success?

_____

_____

_____

_____

In three words, describe what success looks like to you.

_____

_____

_____

What positively amazed you today?

_____

_____

_____

_____

"You are the one that possesses the keys to your being.
You carry the passport to your own happiness."
—DIANE VON FURSTENBERG

Who or what can you place your trust in today?

_____

_____

_____

_____

How would you like your day to be today?

_____

_____

_____

_____

What gives you a sense of peace in the pursuit of your goals?

_____

_____

_____

_____

How has the picture of your goals transformed?

_____

_____

_____

_____

Where do you see yourself in five years?

_____

_____

_____

_____

DATE _____

What tells you you're on the right path to your goals?

_____
_____
_____
_____

How has your pathway to success improved your life?

_____
_____
_____
_____

What effort can you put forth to increase
the likelihood of your success?

_____
_____
_____
_____

Where would you like help to come from today?

_____
_____
_____
_____

If your biggest dream manifested today, how would that feel?

_____
_____
_____
_____

DATE _____

You're driving down the road and see a billboard
cheering on your success! What does it say?

_____

_____

_____

What are three practical benefits of your goal attainment?

1. _____

2. _____

3. _____

What are three ideal benefits resulting from your goals manifesting?

1. _____

2. _____

3. _____

What about those benefits is most important to you and why?

_____

_____

_____

_____

What are you grateful for today?

_____

_____

_____

_____

DATE _____

What is your highest purpose on this journey to your goals?

_____
_____
_____
_____
_____

How has setting your sights on your dreams changed your life?

_____
_____
_____
_____
_____

What successes have occurred that you expected?

_____
_____
_____
_____
_____

What unexpected successes have occurred?

_____
_____
_____
_____
_____

Has your journey toward your ideal life inspired
any positive changes in others?

_____
_____
_____
_____
_____

"Make the most of yourself by fanning the tiny, inner sparks of possibility into the flames of achievement."

— GOLDA MEIR

What new opportunities have presented themselves to help you reach your goals?

_____

_____

_____

Many opportunities appear right where you are. Which have you overlooked?

_____

_____

_____

How has your march to your dreams changed your view of the world for the better?

_____

_____

Affirm three things you are grateful for.

1. _____

2. _____

3. _____

How have your greatest aspirations expanded your vision of what you want?

_____

_____

_____

DATE _____

*Don't be afraid to dream big! What is the
biggest and best thing you seek?*

_____

_____

_____

*Don't forget the small stuff! What little thing
can you make even better today?*

_____

_____

_____

What brought love and joy to you today?

_____

_____

_____

Which big goal are you thankful for right now and why?

_____

_____

_____

Why is your ideal life worth being patient for?

_____

_____

_____

What one thing can you do right now to feel
better about reaching your goals?

_____

_____

_____

_____

_____

What fulfills you today?

_____

_____

_____

_____

Name two reasons you feel confident and hopeful today.

1. _____

2. _____

Where did you find inspiration today?

_____

_____

_____

How will you use that inspiration to further your goals?

_____

_____

_____

What one step can you take right now to move toward your dreams?

_____

_____

_____

_____

**How can you increase your trust that you have
what it takes to earn your goals?**

_____

_____

_____

What would make you even more determined to reach your dreams?

_____

_____

_____

**If you trusted in one thing to bring you to
your dreams, what would that be?**

_____

_____

_____

What gives you a greater sense of your own power?

_____

_____

_____

*"Some days, the most resourceful individual will taste
defeat. But there is, in this case, always tomorrow—after
you have done your best to achieve success today."*
—MAXWELL MALTZ

How did you find success today?

_____

_____

_____

*What happened recently that helped you
maintain focus on your goals?*

_____

_____

_____

What is the biggest thing you are grateful for at this time?

_____

_____

_____

What new goal revealed itself to you recently?

_____

_____

_____

*How do you know you are on the right path
toward your highest purpose?*

_____

_____

_____

What obstacle turned out to be a blessing?

_____
_____
_____
_____

What opportunity did this blessing create for you?

_____
_____
_____

Where can you find direction today?

_____
_____
_____

Name three productive actions you can take today.

1. _____
2. _____
3. _____

What source(s) recently proved helpful?

_____
_____
_____
_____

If unexpected prosperity came your way, how would you utilize it?

_____

_____

_____

**What thought can you affirm today to increase
your feelings of worthiness?**

_____

_____

_____

*How can you be more patient as you wait for
your biggest dreams to be realized?*

_____

_____

_____

What are you asking for today?

_____

_____

_____

Where can you find beauty in your life?

_____

_____

_____

What are the top three things you want?

1. _____

2. _____

3. _____

What makes these three things worth wanting?

_____

_____

_____

*How strong is your belief today that these
three things will come to you?*

_____

_____

_____

What one action demonstrates your belief?

_____

_____

_____

*Who or what can you forgive to clear the
path to reaching your goals?*

_____

_____

_____

"Until input (thought) is linked to a goal (purpose) there can be no intelligent accomplishment."

—PAUL G. THOMAS

Where can you find purpose today?

_____
_____
_____

What in your life inspires you?

_____
_____
_____
_____

Who has been a positive influence on you lately?

_____
_____
_____

Where can you look today for more opportunities?

_____
_____
_____

What happened recently that showed you you're on the right path to achievement?

_____
_____
_____
_____

DATE _____

What insight did you receive today about your number one goal?

_____

_____

_____

What would it take right now for your dreams to manifest?

_____

_____

_____

Where did love and gratitude come from today?

_____

_____

_____

Imagine the success you want. What does that look like?

_____

_____

_____

Have any of your goals changed? How?

_____

_____

_____

_____

What aspect of your goals makes you feel peaceful?

_____
_____
_____
_____
_____

What is it about your goals that makes you feel confident?

_____
_____
_____
_____

In what way does thinking about your goals make you feel grateful?

_____
_____
_____
_____

How has the pursuit of your dreams made you more loving?

_____
_____
_____
_____

How has setting your sights on your goals
made you more determined?

_____
_____
_____
_____

DATE _____

What would be the most delightful thing
about achieving your biggest goal?

_____

_____

_____

What would it take to see even greater successes achieved?

_____

_____

_____

Are you willing to claim these bigger dreams as yours?

_____

_____

_____

Visualize yourself releasing all sense of limitation!
Write a sentence that describes this feeling.

_____

_____

You are now at the peak of your success!
Can you describe where you are?

_____

_____

_____

"This one step—choosing a goal and sticking to it—changes everything."

—SCOTT REED

What are three things you believe in that can help you attain your intentions?

1. _____

2. _____

3. _____

Where can you find support today?

_____

_____

_____

_____

Why do you believe you can achieve your dreams?

_____

_____

_____

_____

Who can you thank today for helping you along the road to your goals?

_____

_____

_____

What delighted you today?

_____

_____

_____

DATE _____

What is your biggest reason to be grateful today?

_____

_____

_____

_____

How will you grow as a person when your biggest goals are reached?

_____

_____

_____

_____

Write one positive statement about your ideal life.

_____

_____

_____

_____

Finish this sentence: "Today I was happy because..."

_____

_____

_____

_____

What would motivate you to put more effort toward reaching your goals?

_____

_____

_____

_____

What issue in your life will be resolved upon
realizing your biggest goal?

_____

_____

_____

_____

What has changed for the better on the path to your success?

_____

_____

_____

_____

What has shown you that you are the one responsible
for making your goals materialize?

_____

_____

_____

_____

If it could manifest right now, what is the
one goal you would wish to see?

_____

_____

_____

_____

What emotions do you feel at the thought of your success?

_____

_____

_____

_____

DATE _____

What was your biggest win today?

_____

_____

_____

With this win in mind, how are you feeling
more determined to succeed?

_____

_____

_____

Where can you look for new opportunities today?

_____

_____

_____

If you follow your heart, where will it lead you today?

_____

_____

_____

What do you need to do to better align your
head and heart with your goals?

_____

_____

_____

"There is no achievement without goals."
—ROBERT J. MCKAINE

What intention can you hold today to keep you pointed in the right direction?

_____

_____

_____

Check in with yourself. Are your thoughts in alignment with your goals?

_____

_____

_____

List five things that make you feel blessed.

1. _____
2. _____
3. _____
4. _____
5. _____

What is the biggest factor that contributed to the creation of your goals?

_____

_____

_____

How do your goals support that?

_____

_____

How can you be more deliberate about your choices today?

_____

_____

_____

_____

_____

What two actions can you take that resonate
with the desired end result of your goals?

1. _____

2. _____

What thoughts can powerfully affirm what you desire?

_____

_____

_____

_____

How do your goals give you peace?

_____

_____

_____

Where do you see yourself 10 years from now?

_____

_____

_____

Write a one-sentence declaration of your intentions.

_____

_____

_____

_____

What excites you today?

_____

_____

_____

_____

What positive change have you noticed in yourself recently?

_____

_____

_____

_____

What single emotion can you express to help you along your path?

_____

_____

_____

_____

**What judgment can you let go of to make
your journey lighter and easier?**

_____

_____

_____

_____

"People with goals succeed because they know where they're going."

—EARL NIGHTINGALE

Finish this statement: "I am a powerful creator, and my dreams are…"

_____

_____

_____

What makes you feel powerful when you think of your goals?

_____

_____

_____

What about your goals gives you a sense of freedom?

_____

_____

_____

What would you like to see today that would pleasantly surprise you?

_____

_____

_____

What can you achieve today to advance toward your goals?

_____

_____

_____

How can you clarify your goals and desires further?

_____

_____

_____

_____

How can you hold yourself accountable today?

_____

_____

_____

_____

Check in regarding your alignment with your dreams.
Do you feel good about it? Why or why not?

_____

_____

_____

_____

What are the most practical steps you can
take today to reach your goals?

_____

_____

_____

_____

How can you dream even bigger dreams today?

_____

_____

_____

_____

What is the most productive thing you can
do today to reach your goals?

What thoughts and actions will increase the
successful manifestation of your intentions?

Where can you find strength today?

Who would you like to share your success with?

Hold the vision of your biggest goal in high
definition. How do you feel?

"I didn't get there by wishing for it or hoping for it, but by working for it."

—ESTÉE LAUDER

What is the most generous reason you want what you want?

_____

_____

_____

_____

What is your current level of willingness to accept your goals?

_____

_____

_____

_____

How can you increase your willingness to trust that your goals will be attained?

_____

_____

_____

Describe your level of gratitude today.

_____

_____

_____

List three things you are grateful for!

1. _____

2. _____

3. _____

What are two positive aspects of your greatest goal?

1. _____

2. _____

How will these enhance your life?

_____

_____

_____

_____

*Name the successes you've had so far and your
plan to reach your remaining goals.*

_____

_____

_____

_____

What other successes would you like to achieve?

_____

_____

_____

_____

*What can you do to let go of any negative beliefs
and increase your chances for success?*

_____

_____

_____

*What will be the biggest feeling of satisfaction
upon reaching your dreams?*

_____

_____

_____

_____

How will you know when you have achieved your goals?

_____

_____

_____

_____

*What was the best insight you learned about yourself when
you realized you have the power to create your goals?*

_____

_____

_____

_____

How will the success you seek bring you peace?

_____

_____

_____

*How will it feel to look back on your old life
once you've found your ideal life?*

_____

_____

_____

_____

"The indispensable first step to getting the things you want out of life is this: Decide what you want."

—BEN STEIN

What did you want to accomplish today?

_____

_____

_____

What source of motivation kept you going today?

_____

_____

_____

_____

Express three things you feel love for.

1. _____

2. _____

3. _____

What event or person has inspired you to work harder?

_____

_____

_____

What progress toward your goals would make you happy today?

_____

_____

_____

List any surprise sources of abundance that flowed to you recently.

1. _____

2. _____

3. _____

What gives you a sense of well-being?

_____

_____

_____

_____

_____

What kindness can you perform today that aligns with what you want out of life?

_____

_____

_____

What kindness would you like extended to you?

_____

_____

_____

Where would you like to see help come from today to reach your goals?

_____

_____

_____

Why is expressing gratitude important to you?

_____

_____

_____

_____

*Why is it important to be open to receiving a positive attitude
and being able to let go of an unworthy attitude?*

_____

_____

_____

_____

Why can wanting something actually become a block to receiving it?

_____

_____

_____

_____

*How can you be satisfied now, yet still successfully
pursue your dreams for the future?*

_____

_____

_____

_____

How can saying, "Thank you," be of benefit in your life today?

_____

_____

_____

_____

"If you don't like the road you're walking on, start paving another one."
—DOLLY PARTON

Practically speaking, do you feel you're on the right track?

Why do you believe your biggest dreams are attainable?

Where can you look today for new opportunities?

Why will making peace with yourself right now help you on your way to success?

Does your attitude reflect your beliefs in achieving your goals?

DATE _____

*How far have you progressed on your way
to manifesting your dreams?*

_____

_____

_____

_____

How do you feel about your progress?

_____

_____

_____

_____

*How can believing there is more than enough for
everyone help you achieve your goals?*

_____

_____

_____

_____

**What do you need to make happen to stay
on your timeline for success?**

_____

_____

_____

What was a source of encouragement today?

_____

_____

_____

_____

What helps you believe you can have all that you want?

_____
_____
_____
_____
_____

How can you best express this belief?

_____
_____
_____
_____

**What needs to happen for you to believe
you can have all that you want?**

_____
_____
_____
_____

What inspired action can you accomplish today?

_____
_____
_____

What do you hope to achieve today?

_____
_____
_____
_____

What three things can you add to your vision of your goals?

1. _____

2. _____

3. _____

How will these three things help you dream bigger?

_____

_____

_____

_____

Why do you believe anything is possible in your life?

_____

_____

_____

_____

Have you encountered any new assets to help you along your way?

_____

_____

_____

_____

Where would you like more help to come from?

_____

_____

_____

_____

How have some of your goals changed?

_____
_____
_____
_____

*How has mapping out your path to success
changed you for the better?*

_____
_____
_____
_____

*How can finding good in something you thought
was bad help you toward success?*

_____
_____
_____
_____

*What positive changes in your life have occurred
as a result of your striving for success?*

_____
_____
_____
_____

How can you show gratitude to the world around you today?

_____
_____
_____

DATE _____

Where would you like to make success happen today?

_____
_____
_____

*How have the people in your life surprised you
with their support as you seek your goals?*

_____
_____
_____

*What specific details can you add to the
attainment of your biggest goal?*

_____
_____
_____

*How can you be happy right now, yet open
to achieving greater results?*

_____
_____
_____

Affirm your three biggest goals now with, "I now have..."

1. _____
2. _____
3. _____

"Every situation, properly perceived,
becomes an opportunity."
–HELEN SCHUCMAN

What steps need to be taken today to stay the course of success?

_____

_____

What other factors could help you along the way today?

_____

_____

How satisfied are you with the progress you've made so far?

_____

_____

What more can you do to increase your progress?

_____

_____

On a scale of 1 to 10, what is your level of trust
that you will realize your goals?

_____

_____

What one thing are you most grateful for right now?

What would make this day great for you regarding your dreams?

What is the ideal way to start each day?

What good do you expect today from your goal-seeking journey?

*Since charting your course to success, how has
your commitment grown stronger?*

Begin your day with three expressions of appreciation.

1. _____

2. _____

3. _____

What is the best thing you can do for your well-being today?

_____

_____

_____

_____

*Where can you look for more abundance and
opportunity today to help reach your goals?*

_____

_____

_____

_____

*How can you give yourself permission to
receive success in all forms today?*

_____

_____

_____

What are a couple of ways you can show love for yourself today?

_____

_____

_____

_____

What is the most important way you can claim
responsibility for your own success?

_____

_____

_____

_____

List two ways you can increase the odds of
creating that which you desire.

1. _____

2. _____

What good news would you like to receive today?

_____

_____

_____

What victories occurred today to help your efforts toward your goal?

_____

_____

_____

_____

On your march to your dreams today, what
would make your spirit soar?

_____

_____

_____

_____

*What grudges or resentments do you need
to release to achieve your goals?*

_____

_____

_____

_____

How can you express love and gratitude for your current life?

_____

_____

_____

_____

*Name three ways you can expand your vision
for your life and your dreams.*

1. _____

2. _____

3. _____

From whom would you welcome encouragement and support?

_____

_____

_____

_____

*What is the best thing that could happen
today to help you realize your goals?*

_____

_____

_____

_____

*What is the best feeling you have today regarding
the work you're doing to realize your goals?*

How can you use this wonderful feeling to reach your dreams?

Are you closer today to your visualized life than yesterday?

**Where and how can you practice patience
today on your walk to success?**

Why is being patient for your goals to be realized important?

"The golden opportunity you are seeking is in yourself."
— ORISON SWETT MARDEN

What is the most powerful, positive source of drive within you today?

_____

_____

_____

What is the most important thing you are grateful for today?

_____

_____

_____

Is your map to your success still clear and concise?

_____

_____

_____

What, if any, adjustments to your goal map are necessary at this time?

_____

_____

_____

How can you own your strengths today to
improve your chances of success?

_____

_____

_____

Describe the strength of your faith in achieving your ideal life.

_____

_____

_____

_____

How can you strengthen this faith?

_____

_____

_____

_____

What have you overlooked in your own backyard
that can help you reach your goals?

_____

_____

_____

_____

If you could ask your own infinite wisdom
for help, what would you ask?

_____

_____

_____

_____

Where can you look for beauty today to
inspire a new level of effort within?

_____

_____

_____

Which of your areas of expertise can help you today?

What feature of your personal power can best serve you today as you pursue your dreams?

How can you be mindful of your goals today?

As you meditate on the vision of your ultimate success, what beautiful images appear?

What is the most empowering thought you can think right now as you contemplate success?

"Opportunity rarely knocks on your door. Knock rather on opportunity's door if you ardently wish to enter."

—B. C. FORBES

What goal-seeking problem can you solve today?

_____

_____

_____

How can you increase the energy of your desires today?

_____

_____

_____

As you look toward your goals, what would bring you joy right now?

_____

_____

_____

What are the three most productive actions you can take today to reach your dreams?

1. _____

2. _____

3. _____

What is the best source of inspiration for you right now to keep you determined and on the path to your goals?

_____

_____

_____

What one question can you ask today to help
you progress toward success?

_____
_____
_____
_____

What answer do you want to receive to that question?

_____
_____
_____
_____

What new insights are you open to?

_____
_____
_____
_____

Are you happy with how far you have progressed toward your goals?

_____
_____
_____
_____

How can you hold yourself accountable today
to make your dreams manifest?

_____
_____
_____
_____

Where did you find a solution to a goal-reaching problem?

What will motivate you today as you seek your vision?

What inner strength is the biggest asset on your road to success?

*What is your inner, wise self telling you to do today
to make progress toward your goals?*

Where can you find a source of purpose to your ideal life today?

"I choose to make the rest of my life the best of my life."
—LOUISE HAY

How would you feel if you were living your ideal life right now?

_____

_____

_____

_____

What are the first three things you would do?
1. _____
2. _____
3. _____

Where would you spend the rest of your perfect life?

_____

_____

_____

Describe the joy you would feel the day your highest aspirations came to be.

_____

_____

_____

How would you feel complete as a person if your dreams came true?

_____

_____

What does success look like to you?

_____

_____

_____

_____

How can you expand your positive thoughts about your goal success?

_____

_____

_____

_____

*Can you look beyond your ideal life to see
more that you can accomplish?*

_____

_____

_____

When you reach your dreams, will the world be a better place?

_____

_____

_____

_____

**How close are you today to reaching at
least one of your primary goals?**

_____

_____

_____

Does the achievement of your dreams have to be perfect?

_____
_____
_____
_____

What if your dream life was even better than you expected?

_____
_____
_____
_____

What will your sense of fulfillment be when your dreams come true?

_____
_____
_____
_____

How do you want to see your successes come to you?

_____
_____
_____
_____

How will you know when you have achieved all of your dreams?

_____
_____
_____
_____

"Our aspirations are our possibilities."
—ROBERT BROWNING

What is your strongest character trait that
promotes goal attainment?

What is your strongest skill that can help you reach your goals?

What is your greatest personality strength
with regard to goal seeking?

What best talent can you incorporate on the road to your dreams?

Is there a latent talent you've yet to tap into to attain your goals?

*With regard to your goals, what positive shift in your
attitude has occurred since you began their pursuit?*

*In what way has the pursuit of your dreams created
a difference in how you see yourself?*

Express your gratitude for three things you have been overlooking.

1. _____
2. _____
3. _____

How have you been true to yourself in seeking your goals?

*What is the first thing you have promised yourself
you will do when you reach your biggest goal?*

*What good thing(s) do you deserve today
to help launch you to success?*

_____

_____

_____

*Why would loving yourself today improve your
chance of reaching your dreams?*

_____

_____

_____

*What practical measures can you take today to feel
better about reaching your greatest dreams?*

_____

_____

_____

What thoughts can help you feel better about achieving your goals?

_____

_____

*How can saying, "I can do this!" increase
your determination to succeed?*

_____

_____

*List your three biggest victories so far on this
journey to creating your dreams.*

1. _____

2. _____

3. _____

*On a scale of 1 to 10, how close are you to
reaching your biggest goals?*

_____

_____

_____

_____

What are two ways you can still improve your plan?

1. _____

2. _____

How do you hope your success inspires others?

_____

_____

_____

_____

*When you are just a few steps from reaching your
goals, how do you envision you will feel?*

_____

_____

_____

_____

Now that you've achieved your goals, how do the results compare with what you've imagined?

_____

_____

_____

_____

How does it feel to have successfully met your goals and challenges along the way?

_____

_____

_____

_____

What is the one thing you are truly grateful for today?

_____

_____

_____

Describe how your dreams and goals are based on integrity.

_____

_____

_____

_____

What will bring you joy today?

_____

_____

_____

ABOUT THE AUTHOR

KARL W. GRUBER has a BA in communications from the
Ohio State University and is a certified Law of Attraction Life Coach.
A runner for many years, he became the ninth man in the world
to run 52 marathons in 52 weeks in 1996–1997, all to raise money
and awareness for and about leukemia. Gruber well understands
what it means to pursue his greatest dreams with persistence,
inspiration, and the belief that one person can make a positive
change in the world. His credo: "Ordinary people can accomplish
extra-ordinary things!"

CPSIA information can be obtained
at www.ICGtesting.com
Printed in the USA
BVHW021056080819
555354BV00005B/19/P